SUPER
SANDCASTLE®
State Stories

FRENCHY'S FLOAT

~ A Story About Louisiana ~

Written by Pam Scheunemann

Illustrated by Bob Doucet

Consulting Editor, Diane Craig, M.A./Reading Specialist

ABDO
Publishing Company

Published by ABDO Publishing Company
8000 West 78th Street, Edina, Minnesota 55439.

Printed in the United States of America, North Mankato, Minnesota
112009
012010

PRINTED ON RECYCLED PAPER

Editor: Katherine Hengel
Content Developer: Nancy Tuminelly
Cover and Interior Design: Anders Hanson, Mighty Media
Production: Colleen Dolphin, Mighty Media
Photo Credits: McIlhenny Company, Natchitoches Area
Convention & Visitors Bureau, One Mile Up, Shutterstock.
Quarter-dollar coin image from the United States Mint.

The TABASCO® marks, bottle and label designs are registered
trademarks and servicemarks exclusively of McIlhenny Company,
Avery Island, LA 70513. www.TABASCO.com

Library of Congress Cataloging-in-Publication Data

Scheunemann, Pam, 1955-
  Frenchy's float : a story about Louisiana / Pam Scheunemann ;
  illustrated by Bob Doucet.
     p. cm.
  ISBN 978-1-60453-922-6
  1. Louisiana--Juvenile literature. I. Doucet, Bob, ill. II. Title.

F369.3.S34 2010
976.3--dc22
                            2009033790

Super SandCastle™ books are created by a team of professional
educators, reading specialists, and content developers around
five essential components—phonemic awareness, phonics,
vocabulary, text comprehension, and fluency—to assist young
readers as they develop reading skills and strategies and
increase their general knowledge. All books are written,
reviewed, and leveled for guided reading, early reading
intervention, and Accelerated Reader® programs for use in
shared, guided, and independent reading and writing activities
to support a balanced approach to literacy instruction.

TABLE OF CONTENTS

black bear (pg. 14)

Catahoula leopard dog (pg. 17)

Shreveport

Bossier City

Monroe

Ruston

plantation (pg. 13)

Natchitoches

Alexandria

steamboat (pg. 16)

Mississippi River

crawfish (pg. 10)

brown pelican (pg. 6)

Lake Charles

Lafayette

Baton Rouge

French Quarter (pg.19)

green tree frogs (pg. 8)

Houma

New Orleans

Queen Bess Island

Grand Isle

Louisiana state flag (pg. 7)

VOTE Frenchy PRESIDENT PSKK

LEGEND

☆ CAPITAL   ● STORY START

○ CITY   - - - STORY PATH

〜 RIVER   ✸ STORY END

Mardi Gras is a big **celebration** before Lent begins. New Orleans is famous for its Mardi Gras parades and balls. Mardi Gras is French for *Fat Tuesday*.

4

FRENCHY'S FLOAT

It was a windy fall day on Queen Bess Island. Frenchy, president of the Pelican State Kritter Krewe, wasn't happy. She was in charge of the Kritter Krewe's Mardi Gras float. The parade was just four months away. Frenchy didn't have any ideas!

"What's wrong, Frenchy?" her mom asked.

Frenchy explained her problem. Her mom said, "Why don't you ask the Kritter Krewe what they think?"

"Thanks, Mom! I'll send them all letters asking for ideas!" Frenchy mailed the letters that very day.

Krewe

A krewe is a group that organizes fun activities for Mardi Gras. It is **pronounced** just like the word *crew*. Each krewe takes part in the parades and balls. Many of the krewes make parade floats.

5

Brown Pelican

The brown pelican is the state bird of Louisiana. It has a huge pouch under its long bill. It scoops up fish and water in its pouch. Then it lets the water out and swallows just the fish!

Frenchy sat on her grandmother's quilt to read the replies. Each krewe member had a different idea! Frenchy couldn't decide what to do.

Then it struck her. The ideas all had to do with different ways Louisiana is great. Each was wonderful by itself. But together, the ideas could tell all about Louisiana! It would be like a Louisiana quilt! They would call their float The Pride of Louisiana.

Frenchy's family was proud of her great, great, great grandmother. She was a beautiful brown pelican. In fact, she was the model for the state flag! Frenchy wanted to make her family proud too. This float could do it! *The Pride of Louisiana* could win the Mardi Gras Gold Award!

Union Justice and Confidence

VOTE Frenchy PRESIDENT PSKK

TICE AND CONF

Louisiana Flag

Louisiana's flag shows a brown pelican feeding its babies. The flag also has the words, "Union, Justice & Confidence." The state colors are blue, white, and gold.

7

Green Tree Frog

The green tree frog is the Louisiana state amphibian. These frogs live around swamps and lakes. They come in many different shades of green! They can be bright green or even olive green.

Tom and Tara Tree Frog said they could make the float base. They live in Lafayette, so Frenchy flew west along the Gulf of Mexico. Then she turned north to Lafayette. She reached their house that afternoon.

Tom said, "Frenchy, we're so glad you're here! We have some old wood to make the float base."

"And we can plant a bald cypress tree on the back!" said Tara.

"That sounds great!" cried Frenchy. After a few days, the base was finished. They all hopped on the float and headed down the road.

Bald Cypress

Louisiana didn't have a state tree until 1963. A fourth-grade class wanted Louisiana to have a state tree. So they and their teacher wrote to the government. They asked if the state tree could be a cypress. It worked! In 1963, the bald cypress became the Louisiana state tree.

Crawfish

Crawfish are also known as crayfish, crawdads, or mudbugs. They look like small lobsters. They live in **freshwater**. The crawfish is the state **crustacean** of Louisiana. It is often used in Cajun cooking.

The next stop was Alexandria to pick up Cindy Crawfish. Cindy's part of the float was all about food. *The Pride of Louisiana* wouldn't be complete without it! Cindy was a Cajun, and she loved to cook.

"Hey! I missed all you guys!" said Cindy. "I've got some jambalaya cooking. You're just in time to have some."

They all ate the jambalaya while Cindy explained her idea. She wanted to include special Louisiana foods. There would be jambalaya, gumbo, and pralines!

Louisiana Jambalaya

1 tablespoon olive oil

1½ cups each of chopped green pepper, celery, and onion

2 cloves chopped garlic

2 lbs. raw shrimp, peeled and deveined

1 28-ounce can tomatoes

1 12-ounce can tomato sauce

1 teaspoon Cajun seasoning

TABASCO® brand Pepper Sauce

3 tablespoons chopped parsley

¼ cup chopped green onion tops

3 cups cooked rice

Ask an adult to help cut and cook the food. Put olive oil in a pan. Add the chopped vegetables. Sauté until tender. Add in the chopped garlic. Then add shrimp and sauté until shrimp begin to turn pink. Then add the tomatoes, tomato sauce, Cajun seasoning, and TABASCO® brand Pepper Sauce. Simmer for 20–30 minutes. Serve over rice. Sprinkle with parsley and onion tops.

Cajun Culture

Cajun **traditions** are a large part of Louisiana's **culture**. The word *Cajun* comes from the French word *Acadian*. Acadians are **descendants** of French colonists that lived in Eastern Canada. In the 1700s, war forced many Acadians out of their homes. Many fled to Louisiana.

11

The next morning, Cindy added her Cajun food to the float. Frenchy said, "Now we're going to see Honey Bee. She lives on a plantation near Natchitoches."

The Kritter Krewe arrived at the plantation house. "Hi y'all!" Honey buzzed. "I've been working on a plantation model for the float. You will love it!"

Natchitoches

The city of Natchitoches was established in 1714. It is **pronounced** "nak-a-tish." It was named after the Natchitoches Indians. The Natchitoches meat pie is one of the official state foods of Louisiana.

12

Tom and Tara helped Honey put the model on the float. "It is starting to look like a real float!" Frenchy exclaimed.

Plantation

Plantations are large farms. Many of them were established in the 1700s and 1800s. Some plantation owners were very rich. They built huge, fancy houses for their families to live in. Most plantations in Louisiana grow sugar cane and cotton.

13

Louisiana Black Bear

The Louisiana black bear is the state mammal of Louisiana. It is a special kind of American black bear. In 1992, it was listed as a **threatened species**. Now there are programs to help the bear's population grow.

14

The Kritter Krewe headed northeast to the Tensas River National Wildlife Refuge. There, Blackie Bear had a surprise for Frenchy.

Blackie had rounded up some new Kritter Krewe members. They were all jazz musicians! Frenchy had never seen anything like it! An alligator playing a saxophone? A flock of birds with trumpets? An opossum on piano? It was wonderful!

Jazz

Jazz music began in New Orleans in the early 1900s. It is a mix of African and European styles. A jazz band includes instruments such as trumpet, saxophone, piano, guitar, and drums.

15

Mississippi River

The Mississippi River is the second longest river in the United States. It forms the border between Louisiana and Mississippi. The first steamboat on the Mississippi River was called the *New Orleans*.

Blackie showed Frenchy a note from Lou, a Louisiana Catahoula leopard dog. The note said that Lou would meet the Kritter Krewe at the Mississippi River. Frenchy said, "That is great! Then we can *float* our float all the way to New Orleans." Everyone laughed. Cindy fixed some food for the Kritter Krewe. Then they all headed to the river.

Lou was waiting for them. He couldn't believe his eyes when he saw the float. Surely it would win the Mardi Gras Gold Award! They loaded the float onto a steamboat. The rest of the trip would be smooth sailing. "New Orleans, here we come!" said Frenchy.

Louisiana Catahoula Leopard Dog

The Louisiana Catahoula leopard dog is the state dog of Louisiana. It has spots like a leopard! Louisiana Catahoula leopard dogs are hardworking and smart. President Teddy Roosevelt had a Louisiana Catahoula leopard dog.

17

New Orleans

New Orleans is the largest city in Louisiana. It is often called the Crescent City or the Big Easy. The French founded New Orleans in 1718. The city is known for its rich **culture**, food, buildings, and music. But it's most famous for the annual Mardi Gras **celebration**.

The Kritter Krewe arrived in New Orleans just in time for the parade. Frenchy added the Louisiana flag to the float. It was finally complete! The parade began, and all the floats moved through the French Quarter.

At the end of the parade, the judges announced the winner. The Pride of Louisiana won the Mardi Gras Gold Award! It was a gold plate that showed the Louisiana state flag. Frenchy looked at her great, great, great grandmother's picture and felt very proud.

THE END

The French Quarter

The most famous neighborhood in New Orleans is the French Quarter. It is the oldest part of the city. Many buildings in the French Quarter were built before Louisiana was a state. The buildings are very colorful. Many have fancy iron **balconies**.

Louisiana at a Glance

Abbreviation: LA

Capital:
Baton Rouge

Largest city:
New Orleans

Statehood: April 30, 1812
(18th state)

Area: 43,526 square miles
(112,104 sq km)

Nickname:
Pelican State

Motto: Union, justice,
and confidence

State bird: brown pelican

State amphibian:
green tree frog

State tree: bald cypress

State mammal: Louisiana
black bear

State dog: Louisiana
Catahoula leopard dog

State insect: honeybee

State songs:
"Give Me Louisiana" and
"You Are My Sunshine"

STATE SEAL

STATE FLAG

The Louisiana state quarter shows a
map of the Louisiana Purchase. The
brown pelican sits on the left side of
the map. A trumpet with musical notes
represents the history of jazz music.

STATE QUARTER

What Do You Know?

How well do you remember the story? Match the pictures to the questions below! Then check your answers at the bottom of the page!

 **a.** jambalaya

 **b.** steamboat

 **c.** plantation

 **d.** brown pelican

 **e.** alligator

 **f.** bald cypress

1. What kind of animal is Frenchy?

2. What kind of tree did they put on the float?

3. What did Cindy Crawfish bring onto the float?

4. Where did Honey live?

5. What animal was playing the saxophone?

6. What did the Krewe use to move the float to New Orleans?

What to Do in Louisiana

1 Look for seashells
Constance Beach

2 See how Tabasco® Pepper Sauce is made
Avery Island

3 Eat a beignet
Café du Monde,
New Orleans

4 Visit a plantation
San Francisco Plantation,
Garyville

5 Ride through a swamp
Prairieville

6 Visit a zoo
Louisiana Purchase
Gardens & Zoo, Monroe

7 Visit a chimpanzee sanctuary
Chimp Haven, Keithville

8 Hear some zydeco music
Cane River Zydeco Festival,
Natchitoches

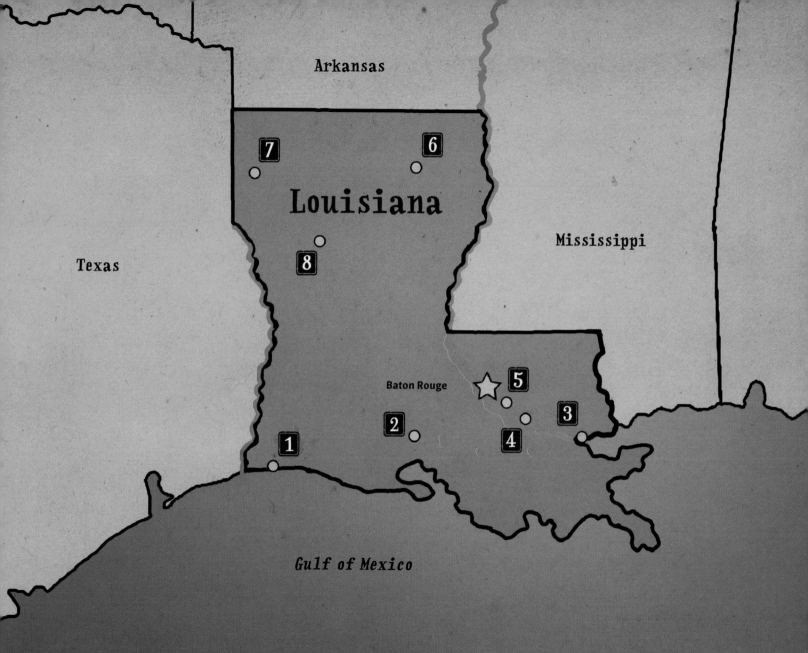

Arkansas

Texas

Louisiana

Mississippi

7

6

8

Baton Rouge

5

2

3

4

1

Gulf of Mexico

GLOSSARY

balcony – a porch with railings outside an upper floor of a building.

celebration – a party or festival held to mark a special occasion.

crustacean – a sea creature, such as a lobster, crab, or shrimp, that has a hard, external skeleton.

culture – the ideas, traditions, art, and behaviors of a group of people.

descendant – people belonging to a later generation of the same family.

freshwater – water that is not salty, such as a lake or river.

pronounce – to say correctly.

species – a group of related living beings.

threatened – when very few of a type of plant or animal are left in the world.

tradition – customs, practices, or beliefs passed from one generation to the next.

About SUPER SANDCASTLE™

Bigger Books for Emerging Readers
Grades K–4

Created for library, classroom, and at-home use, Super SandCastle™ books support and engage young readers as they develop and build literacy skills and will increase their general knowledge about the world around them. Super SandCastle™ books are part of SandCastle™, the leading PreK–3 imprint for emerging and beginning readers. Super SandCastle™ features a larger trim size for more reading fun.

Let Us Know

Super SandCastle™ would like to hear your stories about reading this book. What was your favorite page? Was there something hard that you needed help with? Share the ups and downs of learning to read. We want to hear from you! Send us an e-mail.

sandcastle@abdopublishing.com

Contact us for a complete list of SandCastle™, Super SandCastle™, and other nonfiction and fiction titles from ABDO Publishing Company.

www.abdopublishing.com • 8000 West 78th Street Edina, MN 55439 • 800-800-1312 • 952-831-1632 fax